FOLLOWING DIRECTIONS

Editor in Chief/Project Director: Karen J. Goldfluss, M.S. Ed.

Editor: Eric Migliaccio

Co-Authors: Sara Leman, Eric Migliaccio

Imaging: Ariyanna Simien

Cover and Interior Design: Sarah Kim

Art Coordinator: Renee Mc Elwee

Creative Director: Sarah M. Fournier

Publisher: Mary D. Smith, M.S. Ed.

Teacher Created Resources
12621 Western Avenue
Garden Grove, CA 92841
Printed in U.S.A.

www.teachercreated.com
ISBN: 978-1-4206-8227-4
©2019 Teacher Created Resources
Made in U.S.A.

FIRST CLASS
BOARDING PASS

TEACHER CREATED
RESOURCES

FLIGHT :
95678A

FROM :
LAX

SEAT :
22 D

TO :
JFK

GATE :
O2

SEAT :

TIME :
06 : 30

22 D

0123456789

Dear Parent,

This book is part of the *Practice to Learn* series for young learners. Each vibrant book in the series includes a wide range of interesting activities that will help your child develop essential foundational skills. Written by experienced teachers and educators, the series supports what your child learns at school.

The pages are clear and uncluttered, with activities that build real skills. Activities are fun and motivate children to continue working and learning. Instructions are clear and easy to follow.

We hope that you and your child enjoy using this and other books in the series.

Contents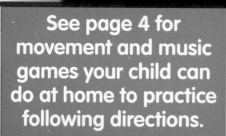

How can you get your children to follow directions the first time and every time? Try turning direction-following into a game.

Movement and Music Games

❶ Animal Antics

Preparation: On one set of about 15–20 index cards, write down action phrases. On another set, write down the names of animals.

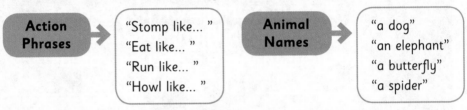

| **Action Phrases** ➤ | "Stomp like... "<br>"Eat like... "<br>"Run like... "<br>"Howl like... " | **Animal Names** ➤ | "a dog"
"an elephant"
"a butterfly"
"a spider" |

Directions: Place the action cards and the animal cards in separate containers. Draw a card from the action container and the animal container in the same turn. Do what the action card says in the way the animal would.

❷ Do As I Say, Not As I Do

Directions: The person who is leading the game (an adult should lead first) gives directions that do not match their movements. In other words, the leader might do the following:

- clap hands (while saying "Hop on one foot")
- shrug shoulders (while saying "Blink your eyes")
- touch nose (while saying "Touch your toes")

The game is about focusing on the movement that is being made and not the words that are being said. Be sure to give your child a chance to be the leader.

❸ Listen and Move

You can also use music as a way to practice listening comprehension and following directions. Here are some great songs to use for this purpose:

- "Walk Around" & "Everybody Clap" by Nancy Kopman
- "Shake Your Body Down" by Laurie Berkner Band
- "Listen & Move" by Greg & Steve
- "Tooty Ta" by Dr. Jean Feldman

Games Across the Curriculum

① Hide and Speak

Preparation: On index cards, write questions or discussion prompts that require a more thoughtful response than "yes" or "no" (but aren't too difficult for your child to answer). Here are some examples:

- ↪ "If you were a superhero, what would your power be?"
- ↪ "If you could drive, where would you go?"
- ↪ "Tell me about your favorite toy/character/TV show."
- ↪ "What is something you wish you could do every single day?"

Once you have written on the cards, hide them. Then, turn your child loose to find them!

Directions: After finding a card, your child should bring it back to you and answer the question before going back to search for more cards. Try engaging the whole family in the game. See who can answer the most questions and collect the most cards!

② Follow that Map!

Preparation: Using a compass, mark the cardinal directions in a room of your house.

Directions: Once the directions are marked, play Simon Says using "North, South, East, and West". For example, "Simon Says take 3 steps east." If there isn't room for this activity in your house, then you can play this game outside instead. Just bring along markers to denote which way the cardinal directions are.

③ What Can You Build?

Preparation: Gather materials such as newspapers, magazines, or boxes into one place. Also, make tape, string, and glue available.

Directions: Give your child a prompt. Choose from the following or come up with one of your own. Be sure to explain any terms or dimensions that your child may find confusing.

- ↪ "Build a structure one foot high."
- ↪ "Build a structure without a base."
- ↪ "Build the tallest structure you can in five minutes."
- ↪ "Build a structure that can fit a toy inside."

Trace and color each shape.
- Use blue for the squares.
- Use red for the circles.
- Use purple for the triangles.

Go Spell Fish

Trace and color each shape.

- Put a check (✔) by each fish that has an uppercase letter.
- Draw a box around each fish that has a lowercase letter.
- Draw lines to connect the letters in the word fish.

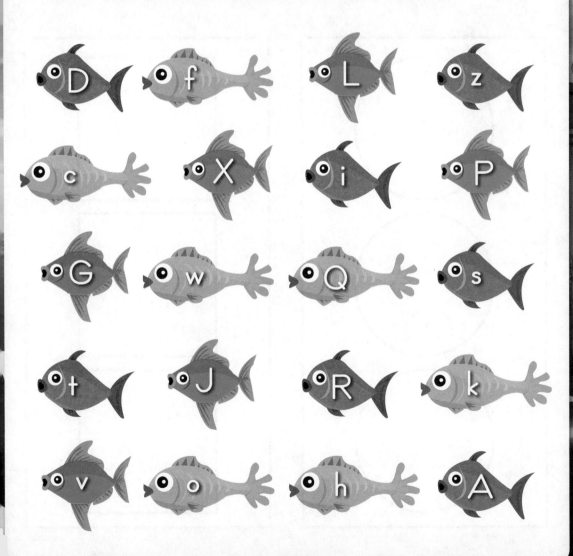

Circles and Squares

Trace and color each shape.

- Color the top circle **red**.
- Color the bottom circle **green**.
- Color the middle circle **yellow**.

- Color the middle square **purple**.
- Color the bottom square **orange**.
- Color the top square **blue**.

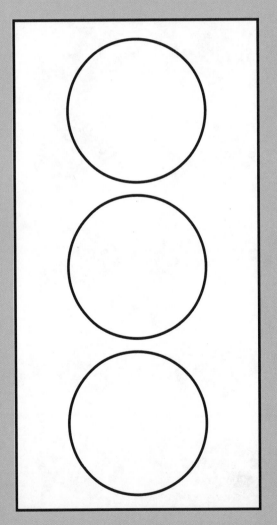

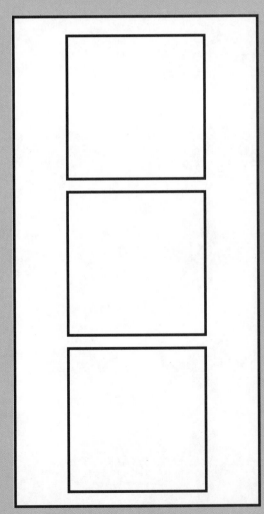

Find and Color

Color each space . . .
- **blue** if it has a circle.
- **red** if it has a square.
- **green** if it has a triangle.
- **orange** if it has a star.

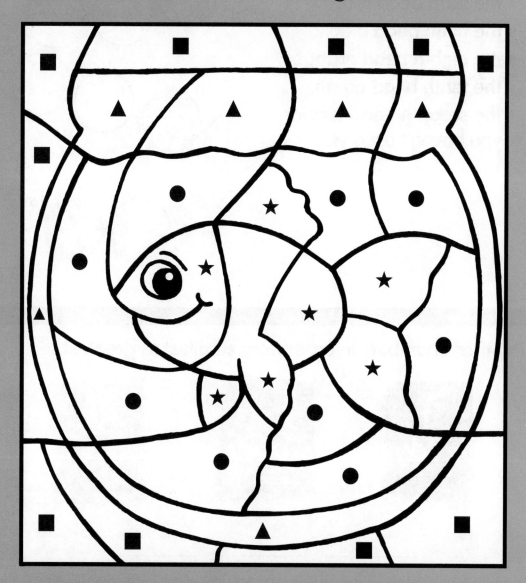

Follow these directions to color the beads.

Color . . .
- the sixth bead red.
- the ninth bead blue.
- the eighth bead orange.
- the tenth bead green.
- the seventh bead a color you haven't used yet.

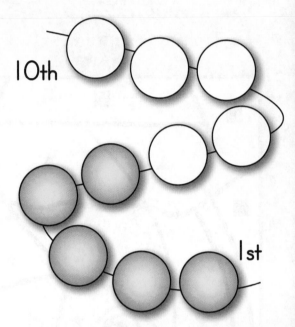

Put these numbers in order from smallest to greatest.

 smallest → _____ _____ _____ ← greatest

Follow these directions to find the mystery shape.
- Cross out the shape that has the most number of sides.
- Cross out the shape that has no sides.
- Cross out any shape that has an even number of sides.
- Cross out all blue shapes.

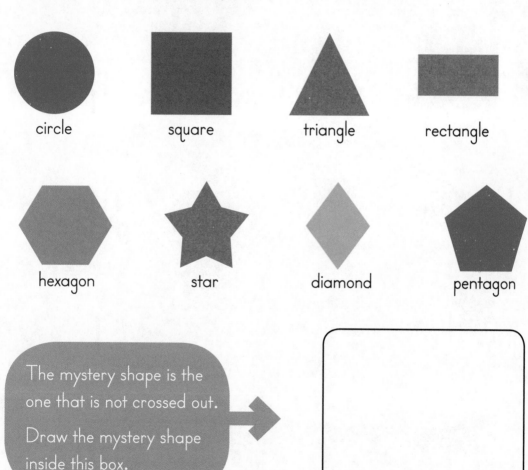

circle   square   triangle   rectangle

hexagon   star   diamond   pentagon

The mystery shape is the one that is not crossed out.

Draw the mystery shape inside this box.

Draw a line from each fish to match the number to the tally marks.

Draw the Line

Look at the information about lines and shapes. Follow the drawing directions below.

straight	————————
curved	
zigzag	

closed shape   open shape

Draw . . .

a straight line	a zigzag line
an open shape	a closed shape

a closed shape
with curved lines

Find three words. Write them in alphabetical order below.

Read the words on the hats.
Write them in alphabetical order.

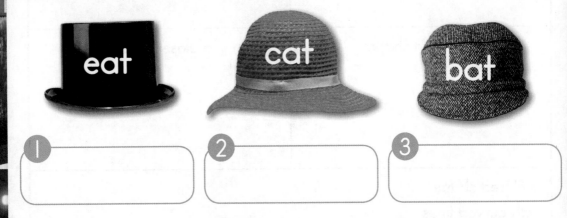

1.

2.

3.

Extra! Circle the hat that has the word that does not rhyme with the other two words.

Better Than Good

Writers use the best words they can. The word "good" doesn't tell a reader much about something. Think of words that are better than "good."

Use a "better than good" word to describe something sweet you like to eat.

Word

Now draw the sweet treat.

Use a "better than good" word to describe a friend, family member, or pet.

Word

Now draw that person or pet.

Rhyme Time

Color all of the words that rhyme with air.

fair

art

rain

share

care

hair

race

mark

bear

Color all the words that rhyme with crab.

car

lab

gab

dab

cab

rob

tab

crib

Kitchen Words

Circle the words that rhyme with mop. Cross out the words that do not.

Use these letters to make words that rhyme with ice. Cross out the letters that do not make real words.

b d j m

n r s z

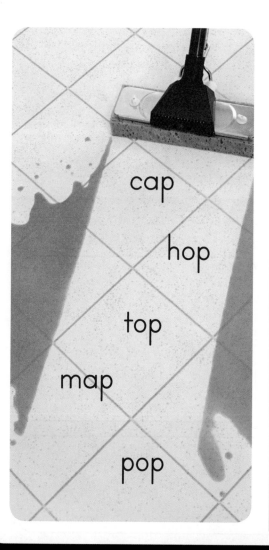

cap

hop

top

map

pop

___ice

___ice

___ice

___ice

Read each sentence. Circle the number words.
Color true or false.

1. A bird has ten wings.

(true)   (false)

2. Dogs have six tails.

(true)   (false)

3. This table has four legs.

(true)   (false)

Draw three cats.

Draw five spiders.

Draw one alligator.

You want to go play with your friends. But before you can go, you have some things to do around the house. You must brush your teeth and put away your socks.

Start by matching up your clean socks. Draw lines to match them by color and the shape on the heel.

Next, brush your teeth. Put the pictures in order from 1–4. Write 1 by what you need to do first.

Finally, rinse your mouth.

Next, squeeze on some toothpaste.

First, wet your toothbrush.

Then, brush your teeth.

Read the words in the boxes. Are they summer words or winter words? Write each summer word on the sun. Write each winter word inside the snowflake.

swim
cold
sled
snow
hot
beach

summer

winter

Can you think of one more word for each season?

Summer: _____   Winter: _____

Read the words in the boxes. On the plate, write the words that name things you eat. On the table, write the words that name things you use to eat with.

fork   fruit   knife   rice   salad   spoon

on the table

on the plate

Can you think of one more word for each one?

food you eat	thing you use to eat with

Days of the Week

Look at the box on the left. The days of the week are written in alphabetical order. Rewrite them on the right. Write them in the order they happen. Start with Sunday.

Alphabetical Order

1. Friday
2. Monday
3. Saturday
4. Sunday
5. Thursday
6. Tuesday
7. Wednesday

Time Order

1. Sunday _____
2. _____
3. _____
4. _____
5. _____
6. _____
7. _____

Bonus: Which two days are in the same spot on both lists?

_____   _____

Months of the Year

Look at the box on the left. The months of the year are written in alphabetical order. Rewrite them in the order they happen.

Alphabetical Order

1. April
2. August
3. December
4. February
5. January
6. July
7. June
8. March
9. May
10. November
11. October
12. September

Time Order

1. January
2. _____
3. _____
4. _____
5. _____
6. _____
7. _____
8. _____
9. _____
10. _____
11. _____
12. _____

Color the beds that have a short e sound, as in bed.

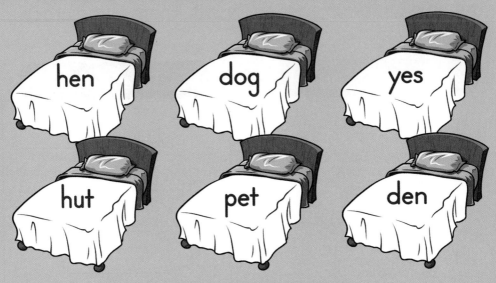

hen dog yes

hut pet den

Color the cups that have a short u sound, as in mug.

tub pot cup

bug sun man

Say each word out loud. Write them on the nose if they have a long o sound.

nose   hole   cot   note   top   rope

Cross out the flowers that do not have a long e sound.

bee   see   pen

red   tree   feed

Letter Treasure

Look at the letter on each coin. If it's an uppercase letter, color the box around the letter purple. If it's a lowercase letter, color the box around the letter orange.

Log On

Look at the number on each log. If it's an odd number, color the box around the number red. If it's an even number, color the box around the number green.

3	7	2	9
6	10	5	11
1	4	14	19
12	17	8	16
13	20	15	18

If the number is less than 10, color the space pink.
If the number is more than 10, color the space brown.
If the number equals 10, color the space blue.

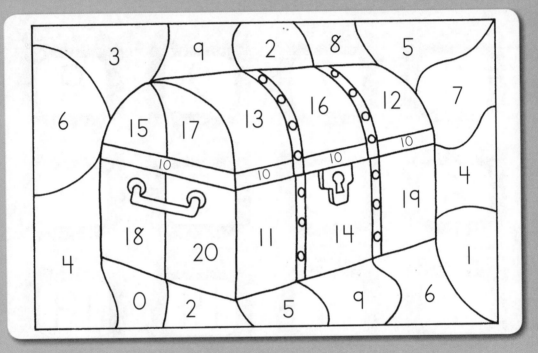

In these boxes, write the numbers 1-10 in order.

In these boxes, write the numbers 11-20 in order.

Number Mazes

Follow the numbers in order from **1–10** to get this bee to the honey.

Follow the numbers in order from **11–20** to get this butterfly to the flower.

29

There is something missing in each picture. Read and draw the missing thing.

coloring book

skipping rope

bicycle

There is something missing in each picture. Read and draw the missing thing.

slide

bubbles

skateboard

Zoo Prompt

Draw a picture of something you would see at a zoo.
Write a sentence about the picture.

_____

_____

_____

Park Prompt

Draw a picture of something you would see at a park.
Write a sentence about the picture.

Look at the blend in the middle of the wheel. Is it a beginning or an ending? It can be both! Add it to each set of letters around the wheel. Make four words from each wheel.

1.

ch _____   _____ ch

ch _____   _____ ch

2.

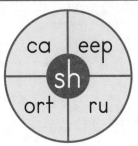

sh _____   _____ sh

sh _____   _____ sh

3.

st _____   _____ st

st _____   _____ st

4.

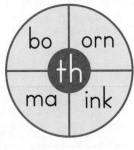

th _____   _____ th

th _____   _____ th

Three and Three

Some words begin with a three-letter sound blend and end with one, too. Use the clues to name some of these "three and three" words.

1. If you have an itch, you might wish you could do this.

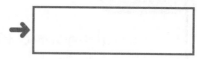

2. If you reach up your arms as you yawn, you have done this.

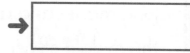

3. You can control a puppet by using these to make the puppet move.

4. This word rhymes with *chills*, and some people get these when they ride on a rollercoaster or see an exciting movie.

5. This word rhymes with *hands*, and it can be used to name units of long, thin things such as hair or spaghetti.

CHALLENGE: Use these clues to find the bonus word.

- **Clue #1:** The word begins with a three-letter blend.
- **Clue #2:** The word ends with a four-letter blend.
- **Clue #3:** The word means the opposite of *weakness*.

What is the bonus word?

Read the story. Draw a picture. Show what the story describes.

Read.

Mo sat under a large tree. Mo had a long tail, a long mane, and a long horn. The horn stuck out of the middle of her head. The tree had four apples that hung above Mo's head. She reached up to a low apple. She gently grabbed the apple between her teeth. Mo loved apples!

Draw.

Describe Where

Look at the picture. Answer the questions below.

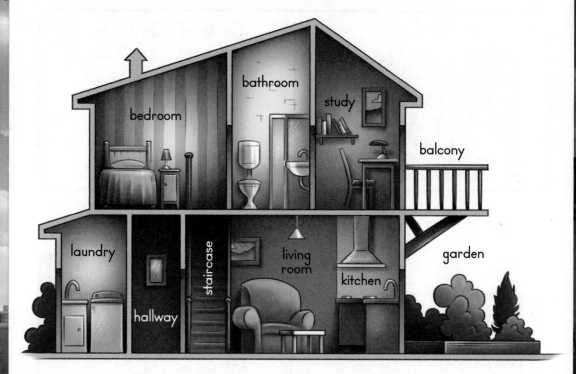

Write two things to describe where the bedroom is in the house.

_____

_____

Write two things to describe where the living room is in the house.

_____

_____

This page comes from a book about the five senses.

My Five Senses

Table of Contents

Use the above page to fill in the chart below.

		Name of Chapter	Page in Book
1.	Matt wants to know about how our ears take in sound. Where should he look in the book?		
2.	Ann wants to know how her tongue can tell that she is eating sweet food. Where should she look in the book?		
3.	Kel wants to know what happens when you grab a hot pan with your bare hand. Where should she look?		

Your Senses

Write three things you can . . .

see

_____

_____

_____

smell

_____

_____

_____

taste

_____

_____

touch

_____

_____

hear

_____

_____

Pictures can make small things look big or big things look small. But in real life, some things are always bigger than other things. Look at the pictures in each row. Circle the thing that is the biggest in real life.

Draw three things. One should be bigger in real life than the others.

Creature Creation

Draw a picture of an animal or other creature. Answer the questions below about your creature creation.

What is this creature called? _____

Where does it live? _____

What can it do? _____

_____

What does it eat? _____

Color By Numbers

The balloons below need to be colored. Solve the problems. Follow the instructions to color each balloon.

The blue balloons have the answer to

$$9 - 0 =$$

The red balloons have the answer to

$$10 - 5 =$$

The green balloons have the answer to

$$12 - 6 =$$

The purple balloons have the answer to

$$11 - 4 =$$

Color Wheel

Use the numbers on this color wheel to write number sentences and solve problems.

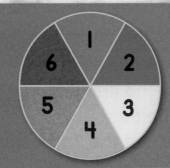

1. red + blue = ?

_____ + _____ = _____

2. purple + yellow = ?

_____ + _____ = _____

3. green + orange = ?

_____ + _____ = _____

4. red − blue = ?

_____ − _____ = _____

5. orange − yellow = ?

_____ − _____ = _____

6. purple − purple = ?

_____ − _____ = _____

7. green + blue + orange = ?

_____ + _____ + _____ = _____

Hidden Holiday

There is the name of a holiday hidden in the message below. Here is how to find it:

- Write the first letter of the message on the first line below.
- Cross out the 2nd letter in the message.
- Then write the 3rd letter of the message on the second line below.
- Continue this pattern of writing letters and crossing out letters.

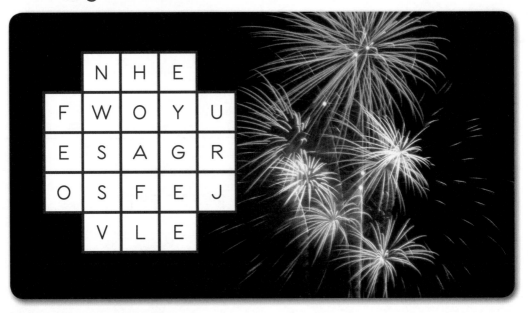

Write the holiday here.

___ ___ ___   ___ ___ ___ ___ ___ ,

___ ___ ___

Use the letters shown to make words. Follow the directions.

1. Letters	
t c a	**Make a 2-letter word.** ☐ ☐ **Make a 3-letter word.** ☐ ☐ ☐

2. Letters	
u b s	**Make a 2-letter word.** ☐ ☐ **Make a 3-letter word.** ☐ ☐ ☐

3. Letters	
a p s n	**Make a 3-letter word.** ☐ ☐ ☐ **Make a 4-letter word.** ☐ ☐ ☐ ☐

The Magic Number

Follow these directions to find the magic number.
Start at 1.

1. Go ➡ 3 spaces.   4. Go ⬆ 2 spaces.

2. Go ⬇ 4 spaces.   5. Go ⬅ 2 spaces.

3. Go ⬅ 1 space.

1	2	3	4	5	6
7	8	9	10	11	12
13	14	15	16	17	18
19	20	21	22	23	24
25	26	27	28	29	30

What is the magic number?

⊕ Make Your Own Magic

Think of a number from 1–30. Then write directions for how to get to that number in five steps. For each step, draw a direction arrow (→ , ← , ↑ , ↓) in the first box. Then write a number in the second box to show how many spaces to move.

1. Go ☐ ☐ space(s).   4. Go ☐ ☐ space(s).

2. Go ☐ ☐ space(s).   5. Go ☐ ☐ space(s).

3. Go ☐ ☐ space(s).

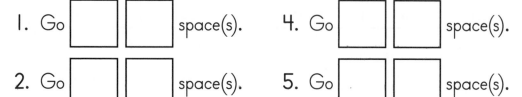

1	2	3	4	5	6
7	8	9	10	11	12
13	14	15	16	17	18
19	20	21	22	23	24
25	26	27	28	29	30

See if a friend or family member can use your directions to find your magic number!

Read these sight words. Then sort them by how many letters they have. Write each word in the correct cloud.

the	with	you	there
from	for	are	have
until	your	about	one

3-letter words

4-letter words

5-letter words

These people need the right equipment to enjoy their sports. Draw to finish each picture.

Give this diver a mask and flippers.

Then add two fish to your drawing.

Give this skater a helmet and rollerblades.

Then add a sun in the sky.

Hidden Animal

Follow these directions to color parts of the grid below.

- Color the box green if it has one of these letters: A, B, C, D
- Color the box red if it has one of these letters: F, G, K, L
- Color the box blue if it has one of these letters: M, N, P, T

A	H	K	P	C
O	M	T	D	R
F	B	S	E	N

Look at the letters in the boxes you did not color.
Write them in order here.

Circle the picture that shows the word you wrote.

Follow these directions to color parts of the grid below.

- Color the box blue if it has one of these letters: T, A, D, J, P
- Color the box red if it has one of these letters: C, K, N, S, Z
- Color the box purple if it has one of these letters: H, M, B, I, G

F	M	N	O	T
P	W	S	D	E
L	K	A	R	H

Look at the letters in the boxes you did not color.
Write them here.

The letters can be unscrambled to make a word. Circle the picture that shows that word.

This dragon is dreaming of things that begin with the letter "D". Can you find all of these "D" things hidden in the picture?

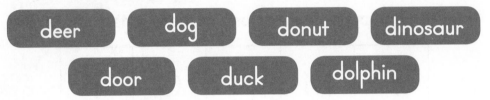

deer   dog   donut   dinosaur

door   duck   dolphin

Color each one you find.

L is for Lion

This lion likes to label things that begin with the letter "L".
Can you find all of these "L" things hidden in the picture?

log   ladder   lamp   light bulb   lips

leaf   lizard   lamb   letter   lock

Color each one you find.

Use this compass to help you tell what is north, south, east, or west.

Follow these directions:

- Circle the picture that is to the east.
- Color the picture that is to the south.
- Cross out the picture that is to the north.
- Underline the picture that is to the west.
- Draw a ball to the south of the sandbox.

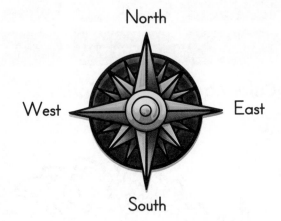

Farm Facts

Choose the best word to complete each sentence below.
Use the words in the Word Box.

Word Box	barn	cattle
	orchard	seeds

On the farm . . .

1. Hay is kept in the _____.

2. Fruit trees grow in an _____.

3. Farmers plant _____ to grow crops.

4. Groups of cows are called _____.

Draw a line from the pictures to the words that describe what you see.

silly

sharp

cold

peeled

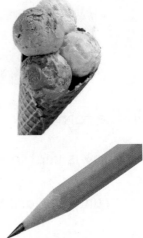

Draw a line from the pictures to the words that describe what you would hear.

drip

crash

fizz

pop

Underline the words that have uppercase letters. Circle the punctuation marks.

Fluff is a little yellow duck. She has an orange beak and big blue eyes. Her feathers are fluffy. She is very cute.

Color the ones that are sentences. Cross out the ones that are not sentences.

Sally sings in the sunshine.

Lots of carrots

a red bow tie

We saw a very big spider.

Can you crack the code and find the hidden words? Use the Code Keys to help you.

Code Key

t = ❀
h = ✚
e = ★
o = ▲
a = ♥
m = ■

❀ ✚ ★ _____

★ ♥ ❀ _____

■ ♥ ❀ ✚ _____

✚ ▲ ■ ★ _____

Code Key

s = ❀
i = ✚
h = ▲
o = ✓
e = ♥
g = ■
w = ◆
r = ●

❀ ▲ ♥ _____

■ ● ✓ ◆ _____

● ✓ ❀ ♥ _____

◆ ✚ ❀ ▲ _____

More Codes

Can you crack the code and find the hidden words? Use the Code Keys to help you.

Code Key

b = ✿
e = ★
u = ✚
s = ▲
m = ♥
t = ■
n = ●

▲ ✚ ●   _____

■ ★ ●   _____

✿ ★ ▲ ■   _____

♥ ★ ▲ ▲   _____

Code Key

y = ✿
e = ★
d = ✚
a = ▲
m = ♥
k = ✓
s = ●

✚ ▲ ✿   _____

✿ ★ ●   _____

♥ ▲ ✓ ★   _____

✓ ★ ✿ ●   _____

Read the paragraph.

Dee needs to go to the store. She needs to buy some food. She needs bread and fruit. Dee will get some butter and some cheese. There is almost no milk in her fridge. She will buy some of that, too.

What five things does Dee need from the store? Write them on the list.

Pirate Directions

Draw these things on Treasure Island.

- a palm tree on the island
- a boat in the sea
- a shovel under the tree
- a chest next to the tree

Color the path of words that begin with s. Get to the treasure.

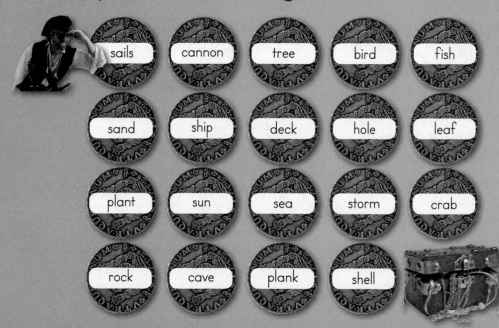

sails	cannon	tree	bird	fish
sand	ship	deck	hole	leaf
plant	sun	sea	storm	crab
rock	cave	plank	shell	

Answers

"Number Directions" (page 10)
smallest to greatest: 37, 43, 56

"Mystery Shape" (page 11)
mystery shape: triangle

"ABC Order" (page 14)
top box: did, hit, sit
bottom box: bat, cat, eat; *eat* should be circled

"Rhyme Time" (page 16)
top box: fair, share, care, bear, hair
bottom box: cab, lab, gab, tab, dab

"Kitchen Words" (page 17)
left box: (circled) hop, top, pop; (crossed out) cap, map
right box: dice, mice, nice, rice; (crossed out) b, j, s, z

"Number Words" (page 18)
top box: 1. false; 2. false; 3. true

"Before You Can Play" (page 19)
bottom box: 4, 2, 1, 3

"Season Sort" (page 20)
summer: swim, hot, beach
winter: sled, cold, snow

"Place-Setting Sort" (page 21)
eat: fruit, rice, salad
eat with: fork, knife, spoon

"Days of the Week" (page 22)
Sunday, Monday, Tuesday, Wednesday, Thursday, Friday, Saturday;
bonus: Monday, Thursday

"Months of the Year" (page 23)
January, February, March, April, May, June, July, August, September, October, November, December

"Short Vowels" (page 24)
top box: hen, yes, pet, den
bottom box: tub, cup, bug, sun

"Long Vowels" (page 25)
top box: nose, hole, note, rope
bottom box: (cross out) pen, red

"Letter Treasure" (page 26)
purple: L, G, T, B, A, C, Z, K, U, M, S
orange: f, d, e, n, w, r, i, h, x

"Log On" (page 27)
green: 2, 6, 10, 4, 14, 12, 8, 16, 20, 18
red: 3, 7, 9, 5, 11, 1, 19, 17, 13, 15

"More Than, Less Than" (page 28)
pink: 3, 9, 2, 8, 5, 7, 4, 1, 6, 9, 5, 2, 0, 4, 6
brown: 15, 17, 13, 16, 12, 19, 14, 11, 20, 18
blue: 10

"Front and Back" (page 34)
1. chew, chip, each, much; 2. sheep, short, cash, rush; 3. start, storm, boost, fast; 4. thorn, think, both, math

"Three and Three" (page 35)
1. scratch; 2. stretch; 3. strings; 4. thrills; 5. strands; *challenge:* strength

Answers

"Describe Where" (page 37)
possible answers: bedroom (upstairs, next to bathroom, above staircase or hallway); living room (downstairs, next to kitchen or hallway, below bathroom)

"Finding Information" (page 38)
1. "Hearing," 8; 2. "Tasting," 18; 3. "Touching," 22

"Really Big" (page 40)
top: elephant; *middle:* ape; *bottom:* helicopter

"Color Wheel" (page 43)
1. 5 + 1 = 6; 2. 6 + 3 = 9; 3. 2 + 4 = 6; 4. 5 – 1 = 4; 5. 4 – 3 = 1; 6. 6 – 6 = 0; 7. 2 + 1 + 4 = 7

"Hidden Holiday" (page 44)
hidden holiday: New Year's Eve

"Word Makers" (page 45)
1. at; cat, act
2. us; bus, sub
3. pan, sap, nap; naps, snap, span, pans

"The Magic Number" (page 46)
magic number: 13

"Sight Word Sort" (page 48)
3-letter words: the, you, for, are, one
4-letter words: with, from, have, your
5-letter words: there, until, about

"Hidden Animal" (page 50)
hidden animal: horse

"What Could It Be?" (page 51)
hidden word: flower

"Which Direction?" (page 54)
circle: merry-go-round; *color:* slide; *cross out:* climbing structure; *underline:* sandbox; *draw:* a ball below the sandbox

"Farm Facts" (page 55)
1. barn; 2. orchard; 3. seeds; 4. cattle

"Sight and Sount" (page 56)
top box: silly—clown; sharp—pencil; cold—ice cream; peeled—banana
bottom box: drip—faucet; crash—window; fizz—soda; pop—balloon

"Sentence Sense" (page 57)
top box: (underlined) Fluff, She, Her, She; (circled) the periods after *duck, eyes, fluffy,* and *cute*
bottom box: (colored) 1st and 4th ones; (crossed out) 2nd and 3rd ones

"Crack the Code" (page 58)
top code (in order from top to bottom): the, eat, math, home
bottom code (in order from top to bottom): she, grow, rose, wish

"More Codes" (page 59)
top code (in order from top to bottom): sun, ten, best, mess
bottom code (in order from top to bottom): day, yes, make, keys

"Shopping List" (page 60)
bread, fruit, butter, cheese, milk

"Pirate Directions" (page 61)
bottom box (colored path): sails, sand, ship, sun, sea, storm, shell

Majestic!

Following directions is a breeze for you!